THE WORLD OF DINOSAURS

ANKYLOSAURUS

BY REBECCA SABELKO

BELLWETHER MEDIA • MINNEAPOLIS, MN

EPIC BOOKS are no ordinary books. They burst with intense action, high-speed heroics, and shadows of the unknown. Are you ready for an Epic adventure?

This edition first published in 2020 by Bellwether Media, Inc.

No part of this publication may be reproduced in whole or in part without written permission of the publisher. For information regarding permission, write to Bellwether Media, Inc., Attention: Permissions Department, 6012 Blue Circle Drive, Minnetonka, MN 55343.

Library of Congress Cataloging-in-Publication Data

Names: Sabelko, Rebecca, author.
Title: Ankylosaurus / by Rebecca Sabelko.
Description: Minneapolis, MN : Bellwether Media, Inc., [2020] | Series: Epic: The World of Dinosaurs |
Audience: Ages 7-12. | Audience: Grades 2 to 7. | Includes bibliographical references and index. |
Identifiers: LCCN 2019003825 (print) | LCCN 2019010541 (ebook) |
   ISBN 9781618916587 (ebook) | ISBN 9781644870860 (hardcover : alk. paper) |
   ISBN 9781618917270 (paperback : alk. paper)
Subjects: LCSH: Ankylosaurus--Juvenile literature.
Classification: LCC QE862.O65 (ebook) | LCC QE862.O65 S237 2020 (print) | DDC 567.915--dc23
LC record available at https://lccn.loc.gov/2019003825

Editor: Betsy Rathburn   Designer: Jeffrey Kollock

Printed in the United States of America, North Mankato, MN

TABLE OF CONTENTS

THE WORLD OF THE ANKYLOSAURUS	4
WHAT WAS THE ANKYLOSAURUS?	6
DIET AND DEFENSES	10
FOSSILS AND EXTINCTION	16
GET TO KNOW THE ANKYLOSAURUS	20
GLOSSARY	22
TO LEARN MORE	23
INDEX	24

THE WORLD OF THE ANKYLOSAURUS

The ankylosaurus was an **armored** dinosaur. Many people compare it to a **tank**!

This dinosaur lived more than 66 million years ago during the Late **Cretaceous period**. This period was the last of the **Mesozoic era**.

Late Cretaceous period

⚠ PRONUNCIATION

AN-kye-loe-SAWR-us

WHAT WAS THE ANKYLOSAURUS?

The huge ankylosaurus was about 33 feet (10 meters) long! Its wide body was covered in strong plates.

Rows of these plates kept its neck and back safe. The armor was tough like crocodile skin!

SIZE CHART

15 feet (5 meters)

10 feet (3 meters)

5 feet (2 meters)

⚠ ITSY, BITSY BRAIN

The ankylosaurus was a huge dinosaur. But it had a tiny brain!

tail club

The ankylosaurus had a small, wide head. Horns pointed out of each side. A narrow beak formed its mouth.

horn

Rows of plates on the dinosaur's back led to a hard club at the tip of its tail.

DIET AND DEFENSES

⚠ ANKYLOSAURUS DIET

ferns

leafy plants

flowering shrubs

The ankylosaurus was an **herbivore**.
It likely ate small shrubs and ferns.
But this dinosaur was not a picky eater!
It **grazed** on most plants in its path.

The ankylosaurus's pointed beak and strong tongue tore plants from the ground.

⚠ SMELLING DANGER

The ankylosaurus had a great sense of smell! This likely helped the dinosaur know when predators were near.

But its small teeth did not **grind** plants very well. The ankylosaurus swallowed most grasses and leaves whole.

BONE CRUSHER

Some scientists believe the ankylosaurus could break its predators' bones with its powerful tail club!

Strong armor made the ankylosaurus a tough match for **predators**. Sharp claws and teeth could not cut through its bony plates!

The dinosaur's tail acted as a defense, too. The ankylosaurus could swing its club tail when in danger!

FOSSILS AND EXTINCTION

Many scientists believe an **asteroid** hit Earth about 66 million years ago. The crash sent up rocks and dust that blocked the sun.

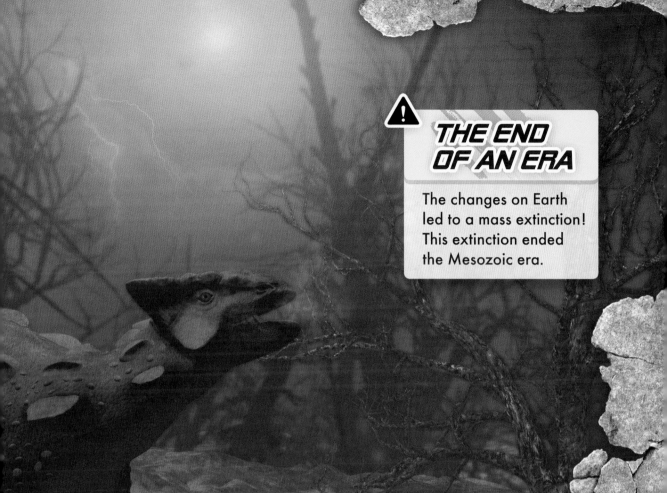

The changes on Earth led to a mass extinction! This extinction ended the Mesozoic era.

Plants could not grow without the sun. The ankylosaurus soon ran out of food.

The ankylosaurus is **extinct**.
But scientists still find clues about its life.
Fossils have been found in the
western part of North America.

fossil of an
ankylosaurus tail club

ANKYLOSAURUS FOSSIL MAP

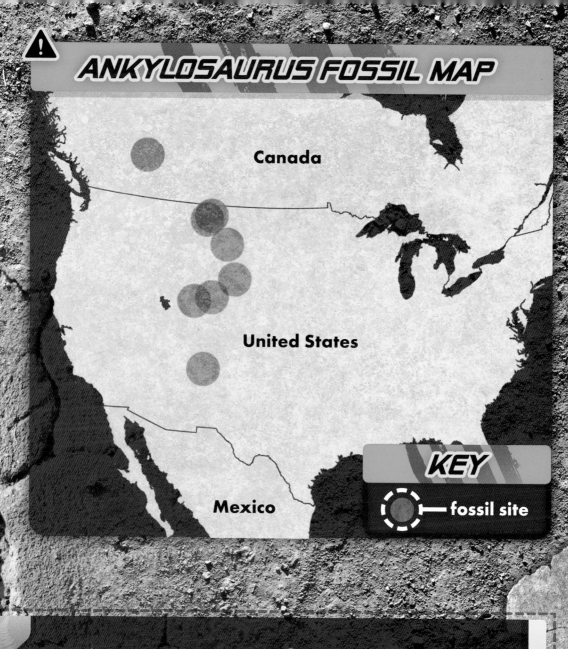

Canada

United States

Mexico

KEY

fossil site

With more digging, **paleontologists** may uncover even more about the ankylosaurus!

GET TO KNOW THE ANKYLOSAURUS

⚠️ **LOCATION**

North America

⚠️ **FOUND BY**

Barnum Brown and Peter Kaisen

HEIGHT up to 6 feet (2 meters) tall at the hip

horns

beak

plates

LENGTH up to 33 feet (10 meters) long

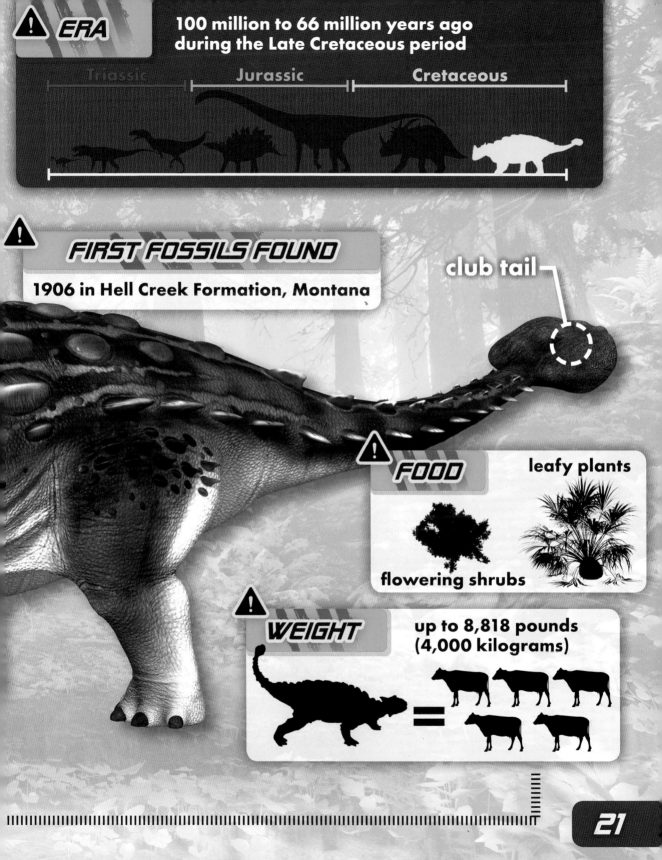

⚠ ERA

100 million to 66 million years ago during the Late Cretaceous period

Triassic | Jurassic | Cretaceous

⚠ FIRST FOSSILS FOUND

1906 in Hell Creek Formation, Montana

club tail

⚠ FOOD

leafy plants

flowering shrubs

⚠ WEIGHT

up to 8,818 pounds (4,000 kilograms)

=

GLOSSARY

armored—covered in flat pieces of hard material

asteroid—a small rocky object that circles the sun

Cretaceous period—the last period of the Mesozoic era that occurred between 145 million and 66 million years ago; the Late Cretaceous period began around 100 million years ago.

extinct—no longer living

fossils—the remains of living things that lived long ago

grazed—ate grass and other plants throughout the day

grind—to break or crush into small pieces

herbivore—an animal that only eats plants

Mesozoic era—a time in history in which dinosaurs lived on Earth; the first birds, mammals, and flowering plants appeared on Earth during the Mesozoic era.

paleontologists—scientists who study fossils

predators—animals that hunt other animals for food

tank—a military vehicle that is covered in heavy armor

TO LEARN MORE

AT THE LIBRARY

Clay, Kathryn. *Ankylosaurus and Other Armored Dinosaurs: The Need-to-Know Facts*. North Mankato, Minn.: Capstone Press, 2016.

Easton, Marilyn. *Dinosaur DNA: A Nonfiction Companion to the Films*. Markham, Ont.: Scholastic Inc., 2018.

Hansen, Grace. *Ankylosaurus*. Minneapolis, Minn.: Abdo Kids, 2018.

ON THE WEB

FACTSURFER

Factsurfer.com gives you a safe, fun way to find more information.

1. Go to www.factsurfer.com.

2. Enter "ankylosaurus" into the search box and click Q.

3. Select your book cover to see a list of related web sites.

INDEX

armor, 4, 6, 15

asteroid, 16

beak, 8, 12

brain, 8

claws, 15

club, 8, 9, 14, 15, 18

extinct, 17, 18

food, 10, 11, 12, 13, 17

fossils, 18, 19

get to know, 20-21

head, 8

herbivore, 11

horns, 8, 9

Late Cretaceous period, 4, 5

map, 5, 19

Mesozoic era, 4, 17

North America, 18, 19

paleontologists, 19

plates, 6, 9, 15

predators, 12, 14, 15

pronunciation, 5

size, 6, 7

smell, 12

tail, 8, 9, 14, 15, 18

teeth, 13, 15

tongue, 12